OLSAT®
GRADE 1
(2nd Grade Entry)
LEVEL B

PRACTICE TEST 1

Copyright © 2019 by Origins Publications

Written and Edited by:
Gifted and Talented Test Prep Team

All rights reserved. This book or any portion thereof may not be reproduced or used in any manner whatsoever without the express written permission of the publisher.

ISBN: 978-1-948255-63-9

The Otis Lennon School Ability Test (OLSAT®) is a registered trademark of Pearson Education Inc, which is not affiliated with Origins Publications. Pearson Education Inc or its affiliate have not endorsed the contents of this book.

Origins Publications
New York, NY, USA
Email:info@originspublications.

Origins Publications

Origins Publications help students develop their higher-order thinking skills while also improving their chances of admission into gifted and accelerated-learner programs.

Our goal is to unleash and nurture the genius in every student. We do this by offering educational and test prep materials that are fun, challenging, and provide a sense of accomplishment.

Please contact us with any questions.

info@originspublications.com

Contents

Part 1. Introduction to the OLSAT® 4

    Who Takes The OLSAT® Level B? 4

    When Does the OLSAT® Take Place? 4

    OLSAT® Level B Overview 4

        Length 5

        Format 5

Part 2. Using This Book 5

Part 3: Test Prep Tips and Strategies 5

Part 4: Question Types and Teaching Tips 7

OLSAT® Level B Practice Test One 15

Answer Keys 33

Bubble Sheets 34

Part 1: Introduction to the OLSAT®

This book offers an overview of the types of questions on the OLSAT® Level B, test-taking strategies to improve performance, and one full-length practice OLSAT® Level B practice test that students can use to assess their knowledge and practice their test-taking skills.

Who Takes the OLSAT® Level B?

The OLSAT® Level B is often used as an assessment tool or admissions test in 1st grade for entry into 2nd grade of gifted and talented programs and highly-competitive schools. The OLSAT® Level B is also used as an assessment tool by teachers to figure out which students would benefit from an accelerated or remedial curriculum.

When Does the OLSAT® Take Place?

This depends on the school district you reside in or want to attend. Check with the relevant school/ district to learn more about test dates and the application/ registration process.

OLSAT® Level B Overview

The OLSAT® is designed to measure an individual's ability to reason logically and think abstractly. Specifically, it tests a variety of skills and abilities in students aged between four and 18, including verbal and quantitative skills and spatial reasoning ability.

The OLSAT® consists of two main parts: verbal and nonverbal.

Verbal questions measure a student's ability to gather and manipulate information from language. They also measure a student's ability to comprehend patterns, relationships, and context clues in order to solve a problem.

To answer these questions, a student needs to be able to fully understand what a question is asking, and make inferences based on what she has heard. A student also benefits from a broad vocabulary knowledge. Although a child needs to understand some verbal language for these sections, all answer choices are shown in a picture format.

Non-verbal questions measure a student's ability to reason her way through non-language based scenarios. These questions take a more visual format, and students answer questions based on information and reasoning from pictures.

To answer these questions, a student needs to be able to find the relationship between objects in a pattern, to predict what the next level of the pattern will look like, and generalize the rules he discovers.

Length

The OLSAT® Level B test has 60 multiple-choice questions. The approximate timeline for the test is 77 minutes (with breaks).

Format

The test is a black and white picture-based exam, and consists of 30 verbal questions and 30 non-verbal questions. Children do not need to be able to read or write to take it.

Part 2: How to Use this Book

The OLSAT® is an important test and the more a student is familiar with the questions on the exam, the better she will fare when taking the test.

This book will help your student get used to the format and content of the test so s/he will be adequately prepared and feel confident on test day.

Inside this book, you will find:

- Overview of each question type on the test and teaching tips to help your student approach each question type strategically and with confidence.

- 1 full-length OLSAT® Level B practice test and answer keys.

Part 3. Test Prep Tips and Strategies

Firstly, and most importantly, commit to make the test preparation process a stress-free one. A student's ability to keep calm and focused in the face of challenge is a quality that will benefit her throughout her academic life.

Be prepared for difficult questions from the get-go! There will be a certain percentage of questions that are very challenging for all children. It is key to encourage students to use all strategies available when faced with challenging questions. And remember that a student can get quite a few questions wrong and still do very well on the test.

Before starting the practice test, go through the sample questions and read the general test prep strategies provided at the beginning of the book. They will help you guide your student as he or she progresses through the practice test.

The following strategies may also be useful as you help your child prepare:

Before You Start

- Find a quiet, comfortable spot to work free of distractions.
- Tell your student you will be doing some fun activities, and that this is an opportunity for you to spend some enjoyable time together.
- Tell your student that she or he should listen carefully to what you say.
- Show your student how to perform the simple technique of shading (and erasing) bubbles.

During Prep

- Before each question, tell your student that she or he needs to listen carefully and pay full attention to the question.
- Encourage your student to look at the answer options while you read the questions.
- Encourage your student to carefully consider all the answer options before selecting one. Tell her there is only ONE correct answer.
- If your student is stumped by a question, she or he can use the process of elimination. First, encourage your student to eliminate obviously wrong answers to narrow down the answer choices. If your student is still in doubt after using this technique, tell him or her to guess as there are no points deducted for wrong answers.
- If challenged by a question, ask your student to explain why he or she chose a specific answer. If the answer was incorrect, this will help you identify where your student is stumbling. If the answer was correct, asking your student to articulate her reasoning aloud will help reinforce the concept.
- Review all the questions your student answered incorrectly, and explain to your student why the answer is incorrect. Have your student attempt these questions again a few days later to see if he now understands the concept.
- Encourage your student to do her best, but to take plenty of study breaks.

When to Start Preparing?

Every family and student will approach preparation for this test differently. There is no 'right' way to prepare; there is only the best way for a particular child and family. We suggest students take one full-length practice test and spend 6-8 hours reviewing OLSAT® practice questions.

If you have limited time to prepare, spend most energy reviewing areas where your student is encountering the majority of problems.

As they say, knowledge is power! Preparing for the OLSAT® will certainly help your student avoid anxiety and make sure she does not give up too soon when faced with unfamiliar and perplexing questions.

Introduction to the OLSAT®

Part 4: Question Types and Teaching Tips

The OLSAT® Level B is comprised of seven different question types:

<u>Verbal</u>

    Following Directions
    Aural Reasoning
    Arithmetic Reasoning

<u>Non-Verbal</u>

    Analogies
    Classifications
    Series
    Pattern Matrices

Following Directions

'Following Directions' questions measure a student's ability to listen carefully and choose a representation (figural design or picture) of a description that is read to a student by a test administrator.

- These questions test a student's knowledge of relational concepts, including distinguishing between and understanding phrases such as "up", "down", "below", "above", "behind" and "next to."

- These questions test knowledge of sizes, shapes, numbers, and letters.

- These questions measure a student's understanding of concepts such as neither/nor, and the order of things, such as first, second, third, etc.

SAMPLE QUESTION:

Which picture shows a black triangle under a black heart and a white star?

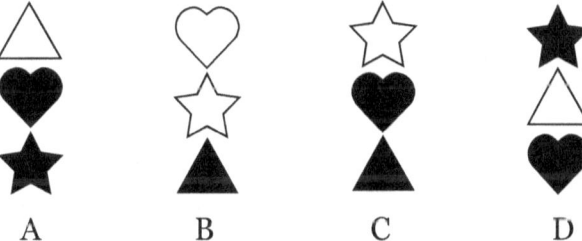

Answer: C

Aural Reasoning

'Aural Reasoning' questions assess a student's ability to listen to, understand and visualize a question that is read aloud to him or her. These questions assess listening skills, visual vocabulary, and understanding about the characteristics and functions of things. They also measure the ability to pay close attention to details, and the ability to use logic and inferences to figure out the correct outcome and response.

SAMPLE QUESTION:

On a vacation, Donna, Rodney and Caroline sunbathed on the beach. Donna and Caroline wore sunglasses, but Rodney used an umbrella to shade him. Which picture shows this?

A   B   C   D

Answer: C   This is the only answer where a boy has an umbrella shading him, and two girls are wearing sunglasses.

TIPS: If your student consistently cannot recall all the information read aloud to her in a 'Following Directions' or 'Aural Reasoning' question, leave out some details that are not essential. Gradually add in more information when you think your student is ready. Aim ultimately to read the whole question just once, as this reflects the actual testing environment.

Arithmetic Reasoning

The main skill tested by 'Arithmetic Reasoning' questions is the ability to create mathematical problems from language and to solve those problems.

- These questions test a student's ability to listen to verbal directions that require him or her to count objects, contrast quantities, and solve problems that involve addition, subtraction, multiplication and fractions with small numbers.

- Some of these questions assess basic mathematical concepts, while others assess more sophisticated concepts such as reasoning and solving word problems.

TIPS: Try using hands-on materials (like blocks, beads or marbles) to help a student become confident with adding and subtracting. For example, you might give your student four marbles and then ask her to "add" five more marbles to the pile. Then, ask her to count how many marbles she now has. This works with subtraction, too.

Introduction to the OLSAT®

Analogies

'Analogies' questions measure a student's ability to reason his or her way through non-language based scenarios.

A student is presented with a 4-box matrix and must identify a relationship between two pictures (or two geometric figures) in the first row. The student needs to apply this rule to the second row and choose which object - from the answer choices - completes this second row relationship in the same way.

The OLSAT® Level B contains two types of analogy questions: picture analogies and figural analogies.

Picture Analogies
To master picture analogies, a student needs to have general background knowledge, a good visual vocabulary, and an understanding/recognition of the following relationships:

Part/whole (or reverse: whole/part)
Object/function (or reverse: function/object)
Agent (person or animal)/location, (or reverse: location/agent (person or animal)
Agent (person or animal)/object, (or reverse: object/agent (person or animal)
Agent (person or animal)/action, (or reverse: action/ agent (person or animal)
Change in quantity, size
Familial -- having to do with family.

SAMPLE QUESTION:

Which image best fits in the box with the question mark?

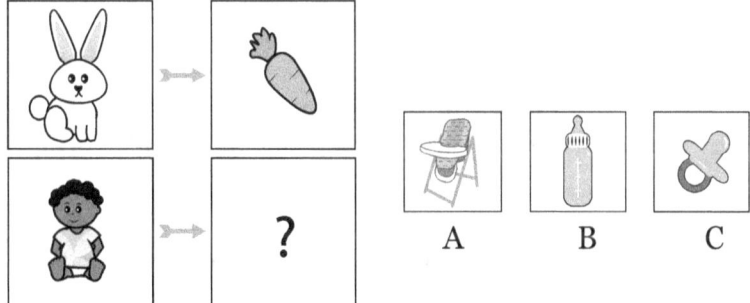

Answer: B: A carrot is food for a rabbit like milk is food for a baby.

Figural Analogies
To succeed on figural analogy questions, student need to understand several key concepts, including geometric concepts such as rotational symmetry, line symmetry, parts of a whole, and opposites.

Introduction to the OLSAT®

SAMPLE QUESTION:

Which image best fits in the box with the question mark?

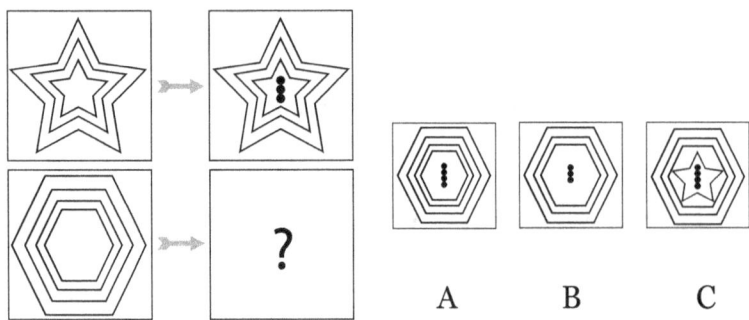

Answer: A The number of dots in the center of the shape in the top right box is the same as the number of layers of the shape in the top left box. The boxes in the bottom row follow the same rule.

TIPS: On challenging figural questions, a student will have to pay close attention to several aspects of the design (e.g.: color, shape, direction) at the same time. With these questions, encourage your student to isolate one element (e.g.: outer shape, inner shape/s) at a time and identify how it changes.

If your student is challenged by these items, ask specific questions to guide him: Ask: "How do the objects relate to each other in the first row? Do you see a pattern or relationship? "Can you guess what the missing object should be in the second row?" Do you see your prediction in the answer choices?".

Classifications

'Classification' questions assess a student's ability to identify what does not belong among a group of objects (figures or pictures). A student has to evaluate differences and similarities among the items in order to correctly answer the question.

- These questions test a student's ability to identify and classify common objects into basic categories by one or more common physical property or attribute (e.g., color, size, shape, weight, liquid/solid, quantity, function).

- These questions test knowledge of common objects and categories, such as fruits, vegetables, flowers, reptiles, mammals, jungle animals, farm animals, tools, furniture, musical instruments, eating utensils, seasons, birds, etc.

Introduction to the OLSAT®

SAMPLE QUESTION:

Which picture does not belong with the others?

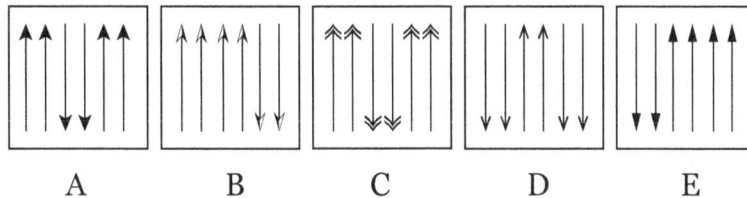

A   B   C   D   E

Answer: D All pictures have four arrows pointing up and two pointing down, except D.

TIPS: Encourage your student to expand on him knowledge of a category in a question. Ask him to name other objects that share the same characteristics and belong to a specific category.

Series

'Series' questions measure a student's ability to predict, according to a rule, a missing element in a series of pictures or figures.

The OLSAT® can contain two types of series questions: picture series and figural series.

Picture series

In picture series questions, students must examine a sequence of objects and identify/predict the object that comes next in the sequence according to the underlying pattern.

Picture series questions test students ability to identify how one or more physical property or attribute (e.g., quantity, size, weight, state (e.g.:liquid/solid), age, etc..) changes over time across the sequence.

Changes include an element or object that is added or removed, that becomes larger or smaller, increases or decreases in quantity, or becomes older or younger,etc.

SAMPLE QUESTION:

Which picture comes next?

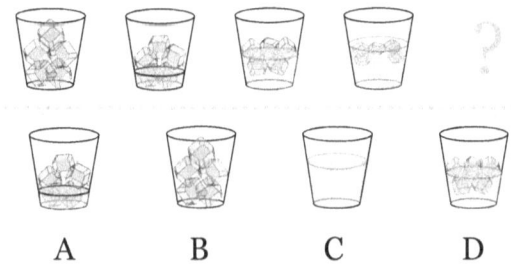

A   B   C   D

Answer: C. The ice in the glass of water progressiviely melts.

Figural series

In figural series questions, a student must look at a sequence of geometric figures, discern a pattern within the sequence, and predict the 'next' drawing/shape in the sequence.

Figural series questions test a student's ability to identify how one or more physical property or attribute (e.g., quantity, shape, size, direction, etc..) changes over time across the sequence.

Changes can include objects or elements getting bigger or smaller, increasing or decreasing in quantity, and/or combining, inverting, or rotating across rows, etc.

SAMPLE QUESTION:

Which picture comes next?

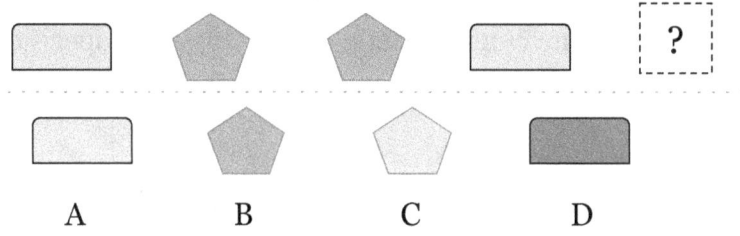

Answer: B

Pattern Matrices

"Pattern Matrix" questions, like series questions, assess a student's ability to predict, according to a rule, a missing element in a series of pictures or figures.

With this question type, a student is shown a series of figural shapes that change across the rows and columns throughout the design. These questions require the child to understand how the objects in rows and columns relate to each other. The student must isolate and apply the rule/s in order to identify which object from the answer choices fits the empty box in the bottom right-hand corner of the matrix.

SAMPLE QUESTION:

Which image best fits in the box with the question mark?

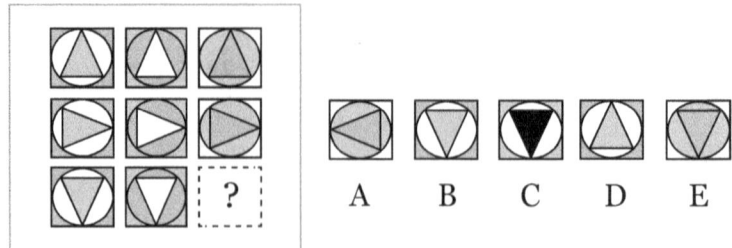

Answer: E

Introduction to the OLSAT®

TIPS: Ask your child to explain what is happening in the matrix, and why he or she chose a specific answer. This will help you understand where your student needs support in understanding the pattern.

Encourage your student to visualize -- observe, imagine and keep track of -- the changes in the geometric shapes as they move and then draw what she predicts she might see in the empty box.

If your student is challenged with a pattern matrix question and finds it hard to detect the rule/s, take a step by step approach.

Encourage your student to discover the rule/s by looking in each direction:

- Horizontally across the rows. Ask: "How do the objects change in the first row? Do you see a pattern? Do the objects change in the same way in the second row? The third row?"
- Vertically down the columns. Ask: "How do the objects change in the first column? Do you see a pattern? Do the objects change in the same way in the second column? The third column?"
- Diagonally. Ask: "How do the objects change across the diagonal? Do you see a pattern?"

Encourage your student to isolate one element (e.g.: outer shape, inner shape/s) and identify how it changes:

- Ask: "How does the color/shading of the element change as it moves along the row/column?"
- Ask: "Does the element change positions as it moves along the row/column? Does it move up, down or around (i.e.: clockwise, counter-clockwise). Does the element move to the opposite position?"
- Ask: "Does the element get bigger, smaller or stay the same as it moves?"
- Ask: "Does the element disappear and appear again as you move along the row/column?"

OLSAT© Level B Practice Test 1

NOTE: The 'OLSAT B' level test is most often given to a child in a one- on-one setting, with the administrator reading the question to the child. In this practice test, you can take on the role of the administrator by reading the question to your student.

Answer bubble sheets can be found at the back of the book. Please make sure your student fills in each of the bubbles fully.

1.

Which image best fits in the box with the question mark?

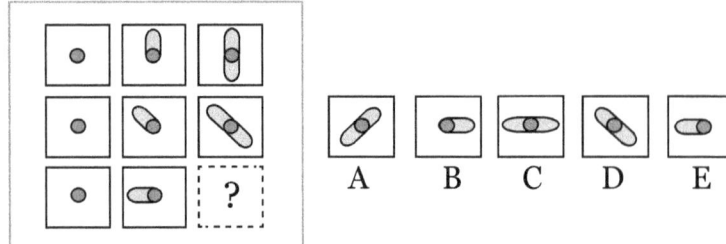

2.

Austin has twice as many ice cream cones as fruit bars. Which picture shows the cones and fruit bars that Austin has?

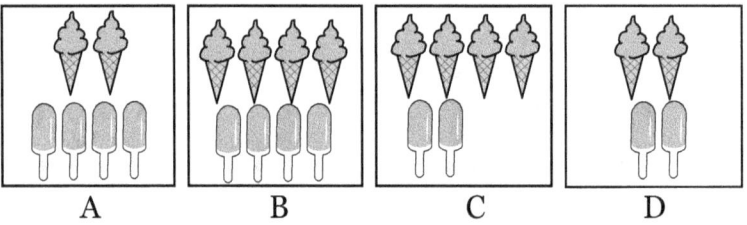

3.

Which picture shows a black triangle under a black heart and a white star?

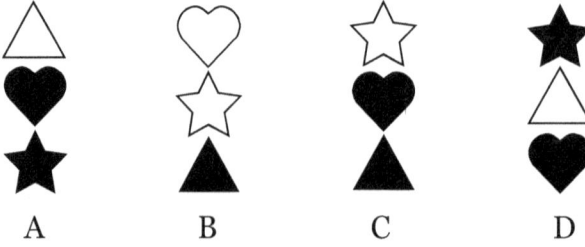

4.

Which picture comes next?

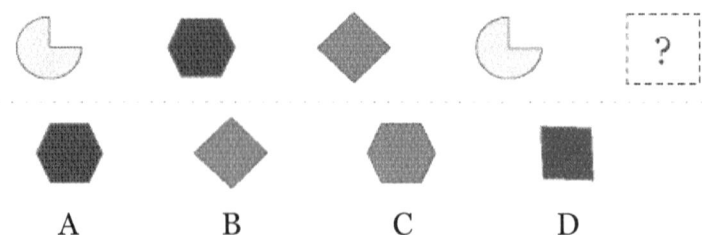

OLSAT® Level B Test Prep Workbook

Origins Tutoring, Inc

OLSAT® Level B Practice Test

5.

Laura wants to give both a fruit and a vegetable to her friends. Which picture shows what Laura should give to her friends?

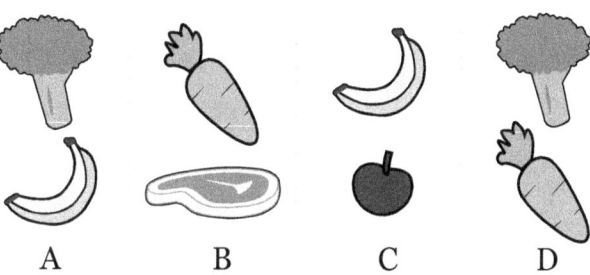

A   B   C   D

6.

Which picture does not belong with the others?

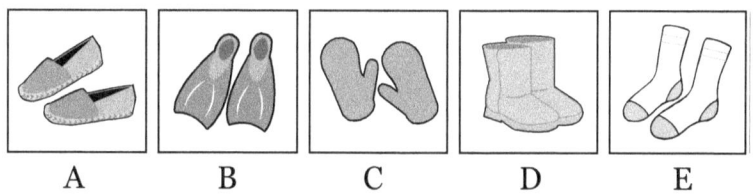

A   B   C   D   E

7.

When Jessie gets home from school she drinks milk, eats a cookie, and writes a note. Which picture show all the things Jessie uses when she gets home?

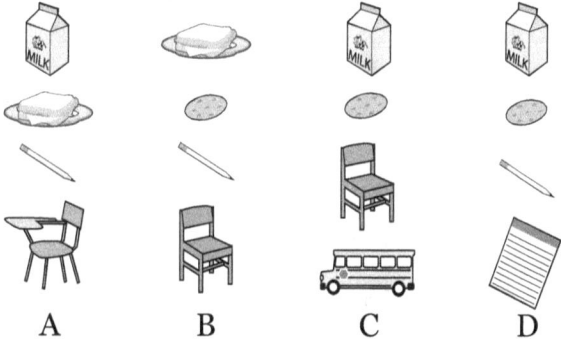

A   B   C   D

8.

The picture at the beginning of the row shows some candies Dara and Chandler want to share equally. Which picture shows the number of candies Dara has if the candies are shared equally?

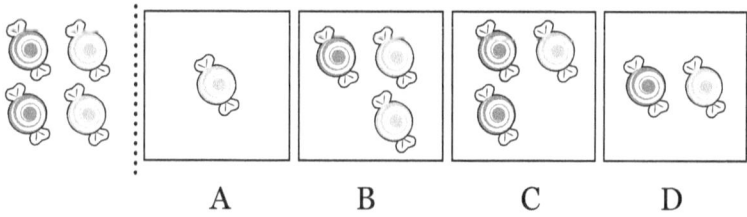

A   B   C   D

Origins Tutoring, Inc   OLSAT® Level B Test Prep Workbook

9.

Which picture comes next?

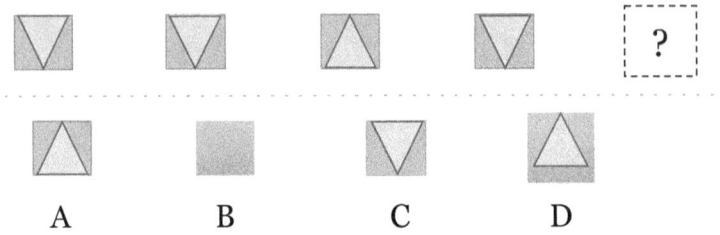

10.

James eats 3 strawberries and a carrot every day. His sister eats fewer strawberries, but also eats a banana every day. She does not eat vegetables. Which picture shows what James' sister eats every day.

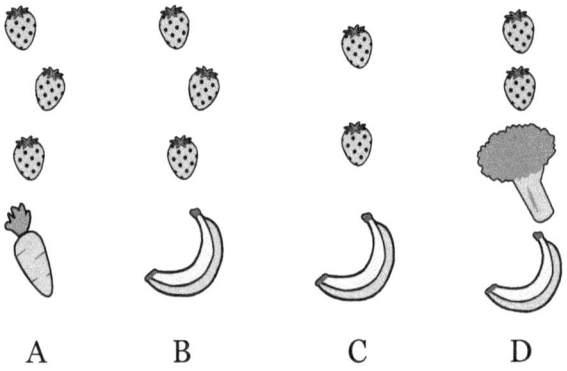

11.

Which image best fits in the box with the question mark?

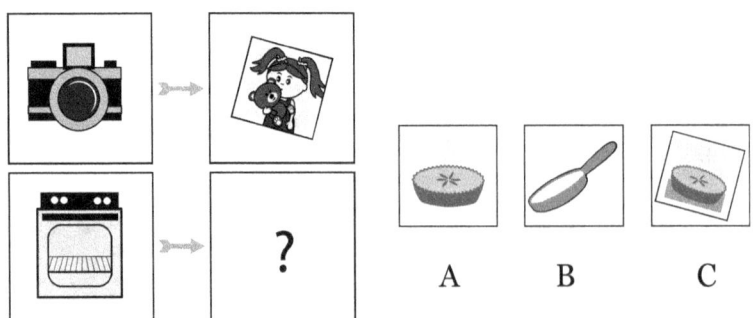

12.

Barry has 2 small turtles as pets. Sharon has 4 large turtles, which you see at the beginning of the row. Sharon lost one of her large turtles and Barry lost one of his small turtles. Which picture shows the total number of turtles that were NOT lost?

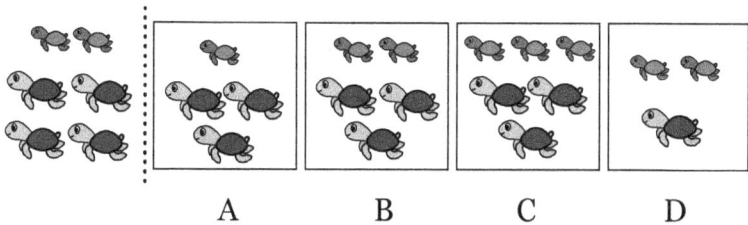

A   B   C   D

13.

Which picture does not belong with the others?

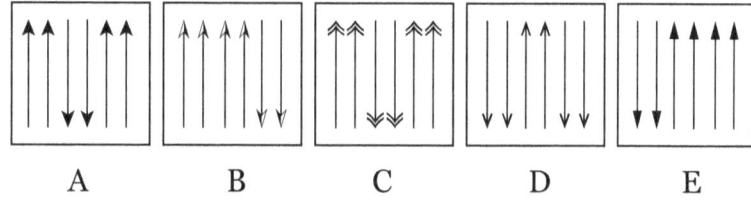

A   B   C   D   E

14.

Mark played soccer and ripped his shirt. Which object should he use to fix it?

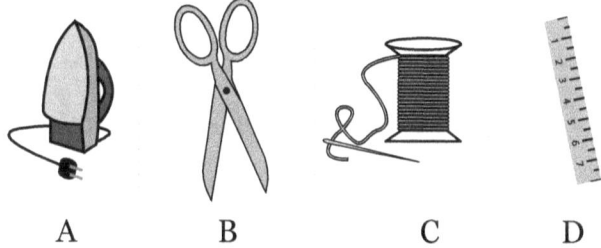

A   B   C   D

15.

Chris and Graham went to the carnival at separate times and rode six rides between them, which you see at the beginning of the row. Graham rode two less rides than Chris. Which picture shows the number of rides that Graham rode?

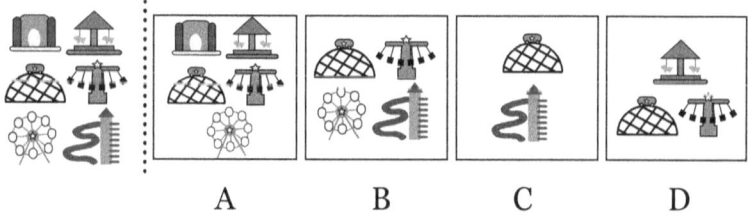

A   B   C   D

16.

Which picture does not belong with the others?

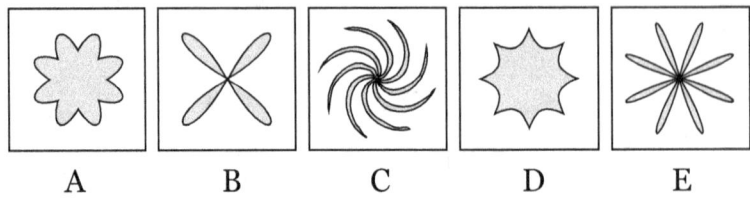

17.

Lauren went to the store to buy an apple, an orange, a pear, and a banana. She forgot to buy a pear. Which picture shows what Lauren bought at the store?

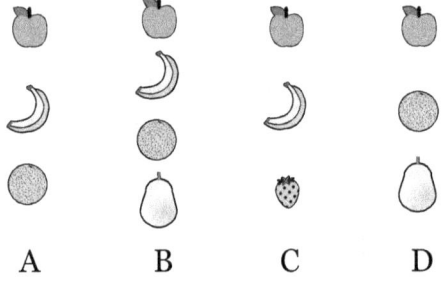

18.

Barry is drawing a picture for his teacher. Which picture will not help Barry draw the picture?

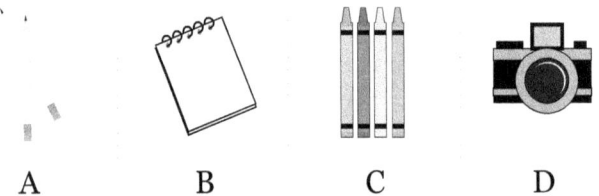

19.

The picture at the beginning of the row shows some snowmen that Becky made in her yard in the morning. Later on, Becky decided to make snowman again, but this time she only made half the amount of snowmen from the morning time. Which picture shows the number of snowmen that Becky built altogether that day?

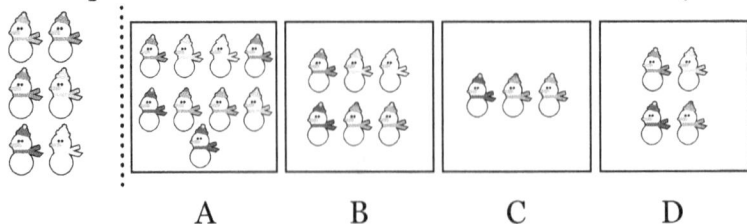

20.

Which picture does not belong with the others?

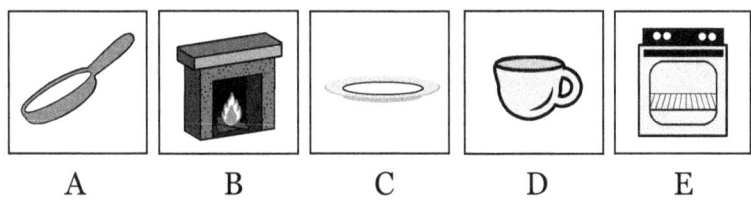

21.

Look at the picture below. N stands for 1 and P stands for 3. Which picture says 1, 3, 1 in this order from top to bottom?

N   **P**   **N**   **N**
P   **N**   **P**   **N**
P   **P**   **N**   **N**

 A   B   C   D

22.

Which picture does not belong with the others?

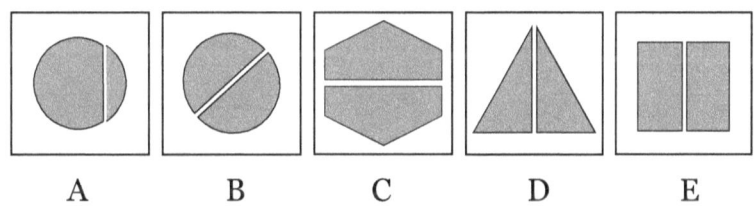

23.

Which picture comes next?

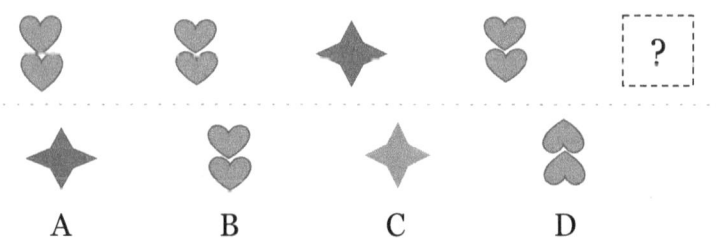

24.

Look at the shapes below. A square stands for 4, a circle stands for 3, and a triangle stands for 1. Which picture says 4, 1, 3 in this order from right to left?

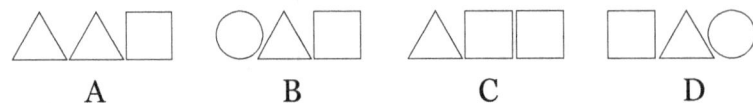

25.

Which image best fits in the box with the question mark?

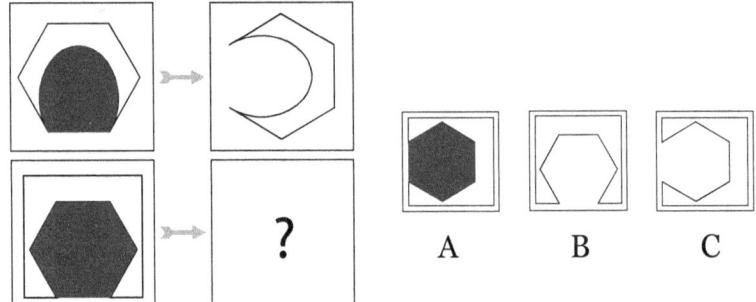

26.

Which picture has a dog above the horse and a cat below the horse?

27.

Which image best fits in the box with the question mark?

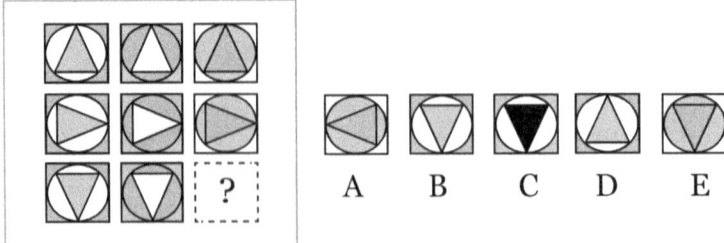

28.

Carmen has some hats, which you can see at the beginning of the row. Carmen gives 6 of her hats to her friend, Jessica. Which picture shows how many hats Carmen has left?

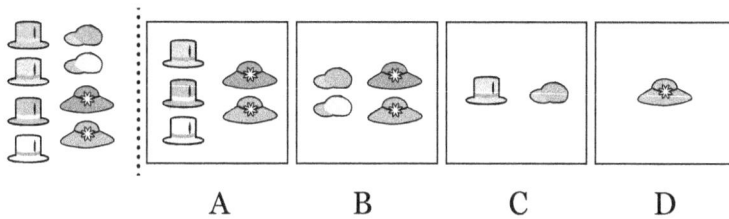

A   B   C   D

29.

Which picture does not belong with the others?

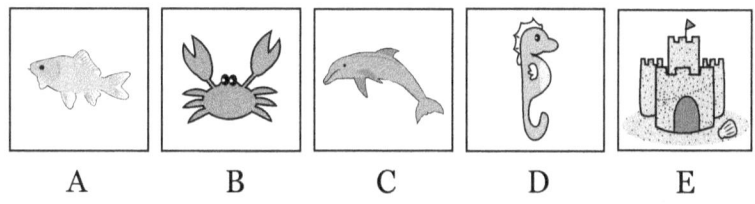

A   B   C   D   E

30.

Johnny wants to score a goal in a net. Which ball would he use?

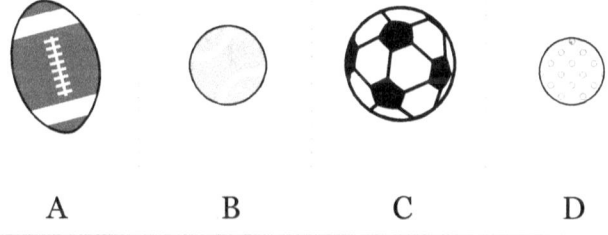

A   B   C   D

31.

Melania has some cups and plates, which you see at the beginning of the row. Patricia has fewer plates than Melania but more cups. Which picture shows the cups and plates Patricia has?

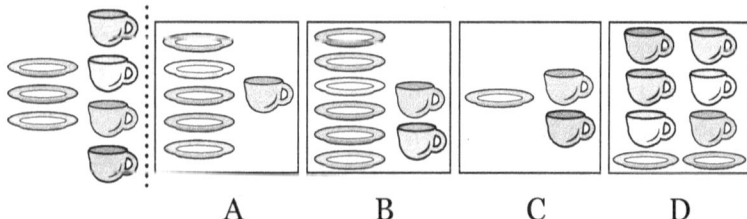

A   B   C   D

32.

Which image best fits in the box with the question mark?

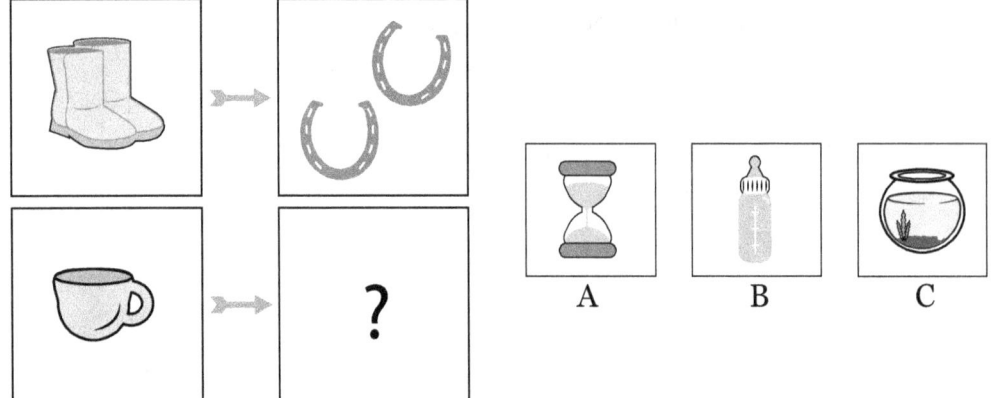

33.

Which picture does not belong with the others?

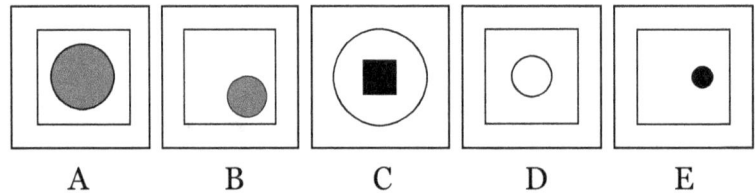

34.

Which image best fits in the box with the question mark?

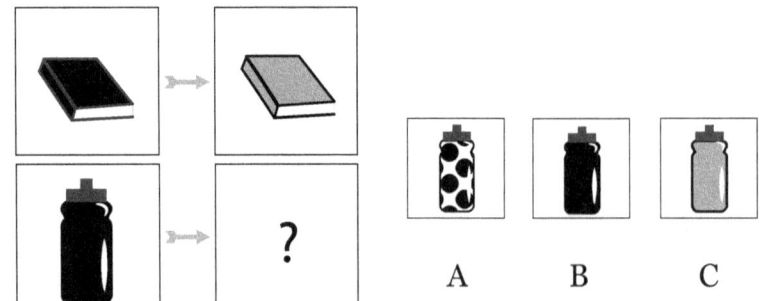

35.

Which picture does not belong with the others?

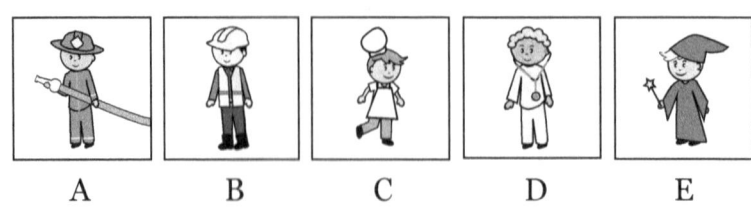

36.

Which image best fits in the box with the question mark?

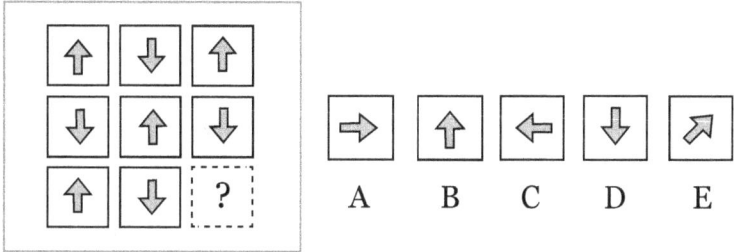

37.

Which image best fits in the box with the question mark?

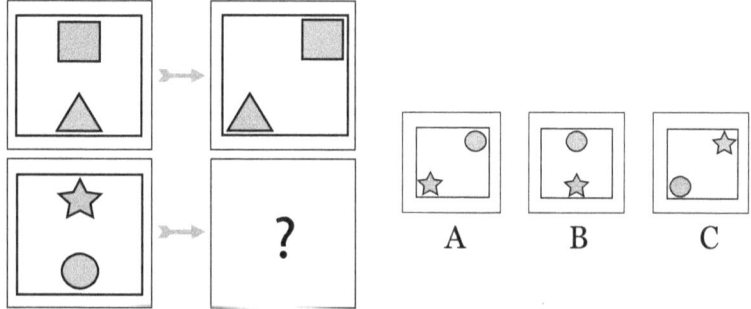

38.

Which picture does not belong with the others?

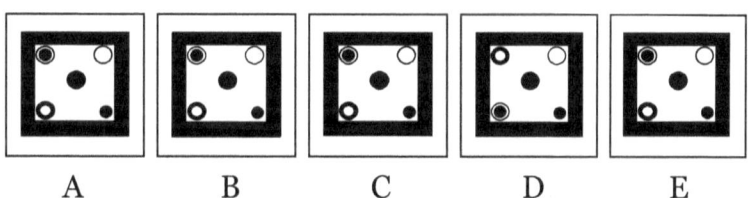

39.

Which picture does not belong with the others?

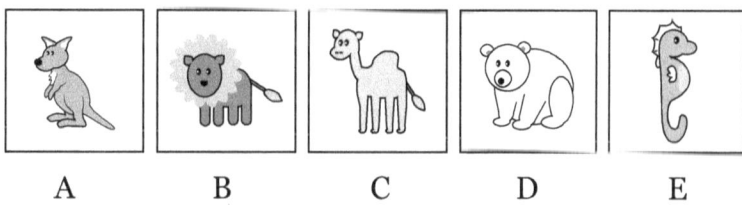

40.

Which picture comes next?

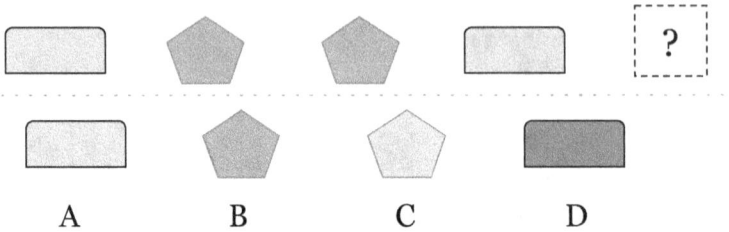

41.

Which image best fits in the box with the question mark?

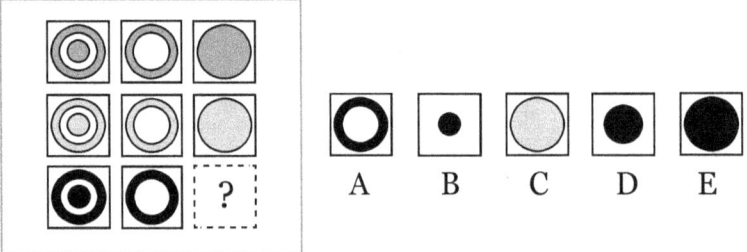

42.

Which picture does not belong with the others?

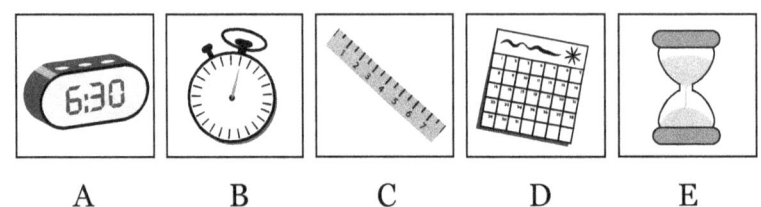

43.

John gave Peter more than six balls. Which picture shows what John gave to Peter?

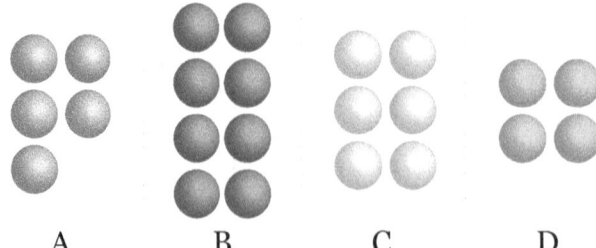

44.

Which picture does not belong with the others?

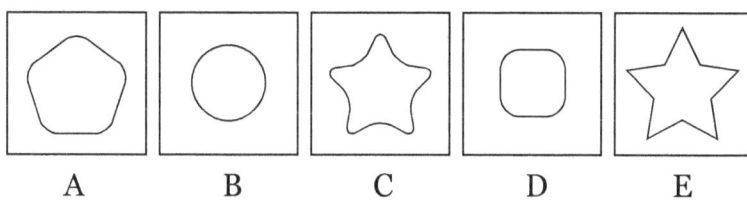

45.

Which image best fits in the box with the question mark?

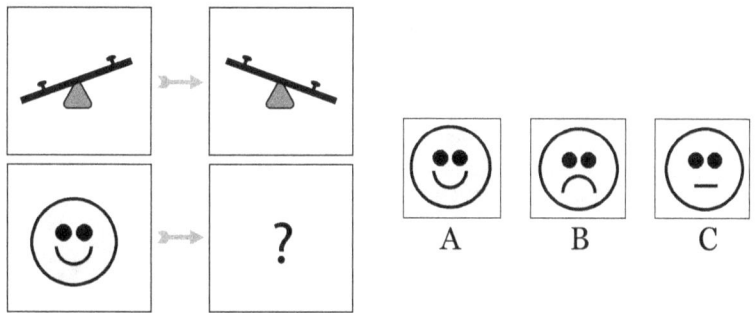

46.

Which image best fits in the box with the question mark?

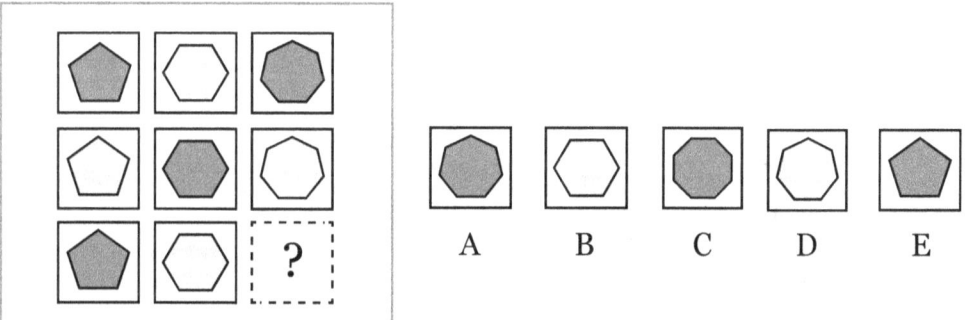

47.

Which picture comes next?

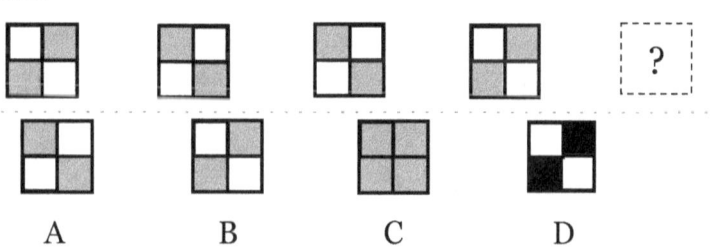

48.

Which image best fits in the box with the question mark?

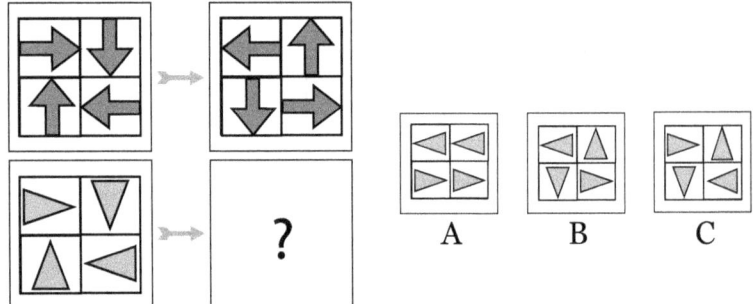

49.

Which image best fits in the box with the question mark?

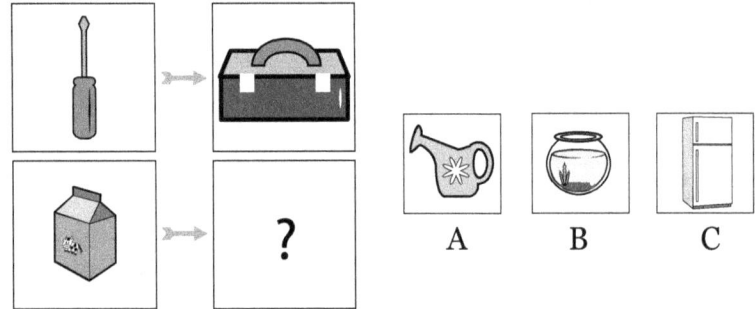

50.

Which image best fits in the box with the question mark?

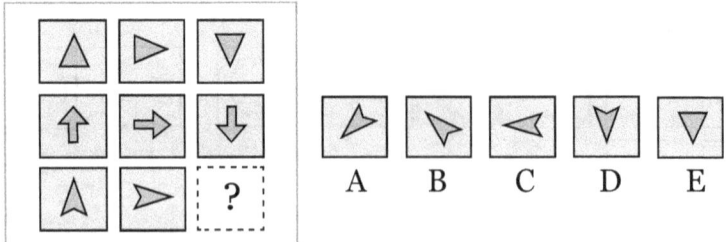

51.

Which of these animals would survive in the Arctic?

52.

Which image best fits in the box with the question mark?

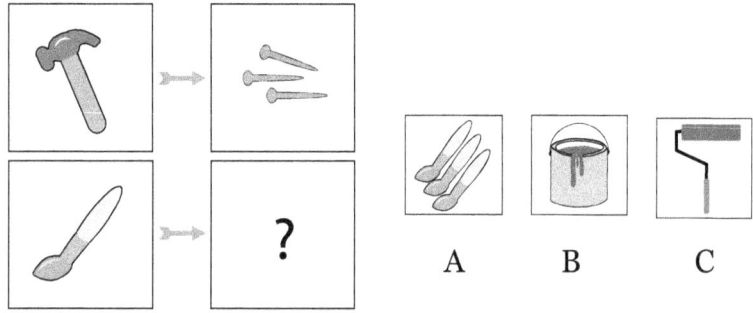

53.

Which image best fits in the box with the question mark?

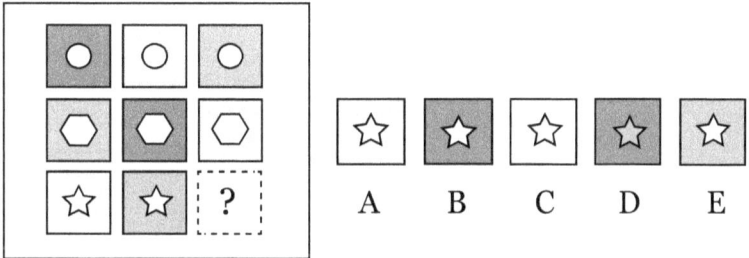

54.

Which picture comes next?

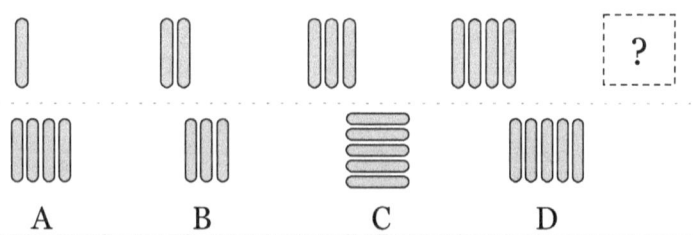

55.

Which image best fits in the box with the question mark?

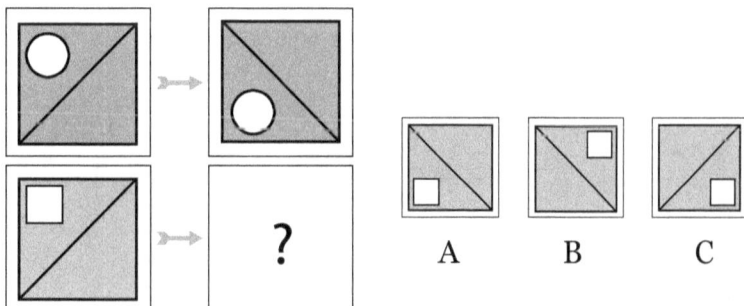

56.

Which picture shows two object that are worn in pairs and used in winter?

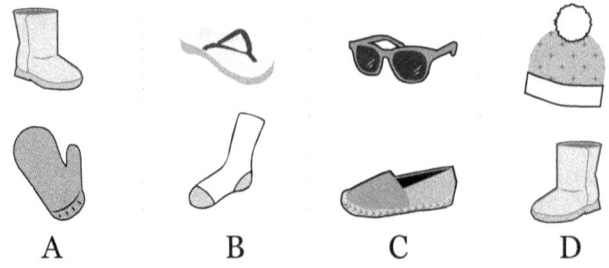

57.

Which image best fits in the box with the question mark?

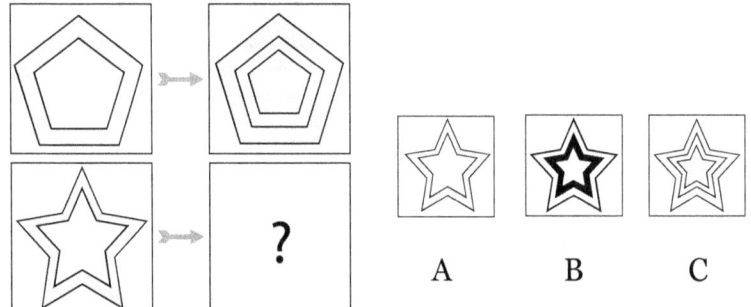

58.

Which picture comes next?

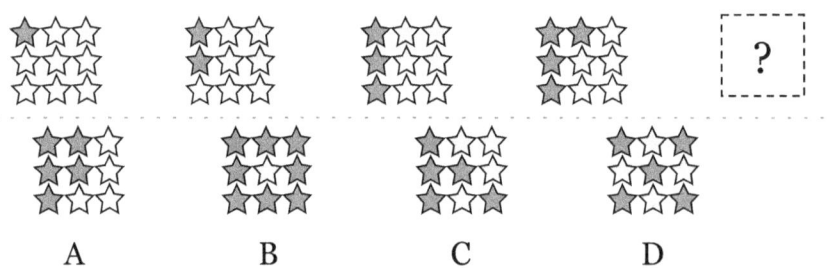

59.

Which image best fits in the box with the question mark?

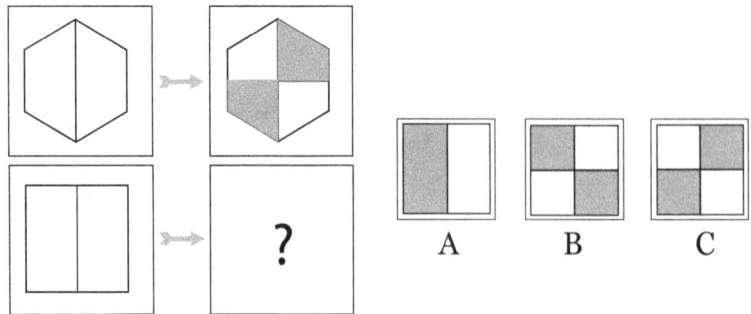

Which image best fits in the box with the question mark?

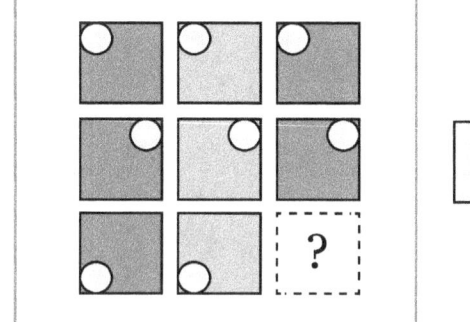 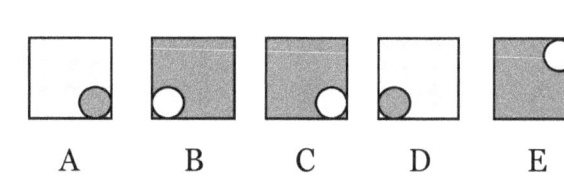

Test One Answers

1.	C	17.	A	33.	C	49.	C
2.	C	18.	D	34.	C	50.	D
3.	C	19.	A	35.	E	51.	C
4.	A	20.	B	36.	B	52.	B
5.	A	21.	C	37.	C	53.	B
6.	C	22.	A	38.	D	54.	D
7.	D	23.	B	39.	E	55.	A
8.	D	24.	D	40.	B	56.	A
9.	C	25.	C	41.	E	57.	C
10.	C	26.	A	42.	C	58.	A
11.	A	27.	E	43.	B	59.	C
12.	A	28.	C	44.	E	60.	B
13.	D	29.	E	45.	B		
14.	C	30.	C	46.	A		
15.	C	31.	D	47.	A		
16.	B	32.	B	48.	B		

Practice Test One Bubble Sheet

> Use a No. 2 Pencil
> Fill in bubble completely.
> Ⓐ ● Ⓒ Ⓓ

Name:_____   Date:_____

1. Ⓐ Ⓑ Ⓒ Ⓓ Ⓔ	26. Ⓐ Ⓑ Ⓒ Ⓓ	51. Ⓐ Ⓑ Ⓒ Ⓓ
2. Ⓐ Ⓑ Ⓒ Ⓓ	27. Ⓐ Ⓑ Ⓒ Ⓓ Ⓔ	52. Ⓐ Ⓑ Ⓒ
3. Ⓐ Ⓑ Ⓒ Ⓓ	28. Ⓐ Ⓑ Ⓒ Ⓓ	53. Ⓐ Ⓑ Ⓒ Ⓓ Ⓔ
4. Ⓐ Ⓑ Ⓒ Ⓓ	29. Ⓐ Ⓑ Ⓒ Ⓓ Ⓔ	54. Ⓐ Ⓑ Ⓒ Ⓓ
5. Ⓐ Ⓑ Ⓒ Ⓓ	30. Ⓐ Ⓑ Ⓒ Ⓓ	55. Ⓐ Ⓑ Ⓒ
6. Ⓐ Ⓑ Ⓒ Ⓓ Ⓔ	31. Ⓐ Ⓑ Ⓒ Ⓓ Ⓔ	56. Ⓐ Ⓑ Ⓒ Ⓓ
7. Ⓐ Ⓑ Ⓒ Ⓓ	32. Ⓐ Ⓑ Ⓒ	57. Ⓐ Ⓑ Ⓒ
8. Ⓐ Ⓑ Ⓒ Ⓓ	33. Ⓐ Ⓑ Ⓒ Ⓓ Ⓔ	58. Ⓐ Ⓑ Ⓒ Ⓓ
9. Ⓐ Ⓑ Ⓒ Ⓓ	34. Ⓐ Ⓑ Ⓒ	59. Ⓐ Ⓑ Ⓒ
10. Ⓐ Ⓑ Ⓒ Ⓓ	35. Ⓐ Ⓑ Ⓒ Ⓓ Ⓔ	60. Ⓐ Ⓑ Ⓒ Ⓓ Ⓔ
11. Ⓐ Ⓑ Ⓒ	36. Ⓐ Ⓑ Ⓒ Ⓓ Ⓔ	
12. Ⓐ Ⓑ Ⓒ Ⓓ	37. Ⓐ Ⓑ Ⓒ	
13. Ⓐ Ⓑ Ⓒ Ⓓ Ⓔ	38. Ⓐ Ⓑ Ⓒ Ⓓ Ⓔ	
14. Ⓐ Ⓑ Ⓒ Ⓓ	39. Ⓐ Ⓑ Ⓒ Ⓓ Ⓔ	
15. Ⓐ Ⓑ Ⓒ Ⓓ	40. Ⓐ Ⓑ Ⓒ Ⓓ	
16. Ⓐ Ⓑ Ⓒ Ⓓ Ⓔ	41. Ⓐ Ⓑ Ⓒ Ⓓ Ⓔ	
17. Ⓐ Ⓑ Ⓒ Ⓓ	42. Ⓐ Ⓑ Ⓒ Ⓓ Ⓔ	
18. Ⓐ Ⓑ Ⓒ Ⓓ	43. Ⓐ Ⓑ Ⓒ Ⓓ	
19. Ⓐ Ⓑ Ⓒ Ⓓ	44. Ⓐ Ⓑ Ⓒ Ⓓ Ⓔ	
20. Ⓐ Ⓑ Ⓒ Ⓓ Ⓔ	45. Ⓐ Ⓑ Ⓒ	
21. Ⓐ Ⓑ Ⓒ Ⓓ	46. Ⓐ Ⓑ Ⓒ Ⓓ Ⓔ	
22. Ⓐ Ⓑ Ⓒ Ⓓ Ⓔ	47. Ⓐ Ⓑ Ⓒ Ⓓ	
23. Ⓐ Ⓑ Ⓒ Ⓓ	48. Ⓐ Ⓑ Ⓒ	
24. Ⓐ Ⓑ Ⓒ Ⓓ	49. Ⓐ Ⓑ Ⓒ	
25. Ⓐ Ⓑ Ⓒ	50. Ⓐ Ⓑ Ⓒ Ⓓ Ⓔ	

www.ingramcontent.com/pod-product-compliance
Lightning Source LLC
Chambersburg PA
CBHW080024130526
44591CB00036B/2643